RECORD
OF ORAL
LANGUAGE

RECORD OF ORAL LANGUAGE

Observing Changes in the Acquisition of Language Structures

A GUIDE FOR TEACHING

Marie M. Clay, Malcolm Gill, Ted Glynn,
Tony McNaughton, Keith Salmon

Published by Heinemann Education, a division of Reed Publishing (NZ) Ltd, 39 Rawene Road, Birkenhead, Auckland, New Zealand. Associated companies, branches and representatives throughout the world.

In the United States: Heinemann, a division of Reed Elsevier Inc. (USA), 361 Hanover Street, Portsmouth, NH 03801-3912.

ISBN-13: 978-1-86970-599-2 (NZ)
ISBN-10: 1-86970-599-8 (NZ)
© 2007 The Marie Clay Literacy Trust, et al

Record of Oral Language was first published in 1976 by New Zealand Educational Institute. In 1983 it was published in an edition with *Biks and Gutches*.

Library of Congress Cataloguing-in-Publication Data
CIP data is on file with the Library of Congress
ISBN: 0-325-01292-x
ISBN-13: 978-0-325-01292-6
Global ID: E01292

Cover design by Brenda Cantell
Cover illustration by Sandra Cammell

Printed in China by Nordica

The pronouns 'she' and 'he' have often been used in this text to refer to the teacher and child respectively. Despite a possible charge of sexist bias it makes for clearer, easier reading if such references are consistent.

Contents

For a quick but valid check on a child's knowledge of language structure

Record the most complex sentence you have heard this child construct in a conversation in the past week. Check at intervals and replace that example with the next most complex sentence you hear. (If you understand linguistics, count the number of morphemes.)

Preface

This book describes a technique for observing one aspect of language development. It was developed for research studies of young children from three ethnic groups in New Zealand. Experience has shown that it helps practising teachers to observe and understand changes in young children's language. The book is directed towards teachers who wish to do this.

Asking children to repeat some sentences and listening carefully to their attempts can sharpen teachers' hearing of what children say, and improve the accuracy of the records they make. The child is asked to repeat a set of sentences that are graded for difficulty. Students of linguistics who are trained to identify linguistic structures and morphological rules will recognise that the language forms used in these tasks come from linguistic descriptions of English. It is not necessary for observers to understand these linguistic descriptions before using the techniques: the task should make them more sensitive to the nature of a particular child's use of English.

Young children's control of English is assumed to increase gradually over most of their school years. The changes occurring can be monitored through the use of this 'Record of Oral Language' and of another assessment called 'Biks and Gutches', which you will find in a companion volume (Clay, 2007). Teachers could judge from either or both of these assessments which children have made poor, average or good progress in two aspects of development.

These techniques are appropriate

+ for children of four to seven years of age with English as a mother tongue,
+ and, for five years after children begin to learn English as another language.

Performance on these tasks can be used to select children for more intensive attention to oral language learning or to check what changes have occurred in children's language as a result of particular instruction. Change over time can be an important indicator of whether a particular child will know how to learn more about language for themselves in the future.

These observation tasks have been developed and tested as if they were normative, standardised tests.

+ The difficulty of the items,
+ the reliability of the total scores,
+ the sampling of language behaviours,
+ the suitability of the tasks for the age-group concerned,

were each carefully assessed. Evidence is presented in the technical appendices. Although normative scores were available on satisfactory samples of New Zealand children, it was decided that these would not be published. One reason was that despite remarkable consistency in the difficulty level of the sentences in the Record of Oral Language it was suspected that scores could vary markedly from one group of children to another depending on their previous opportunities to learn the language. Instead of normative scores it is suggested that any particular school or group keep a record of the range of scores gained by children in that school, and work out the averages for their own groups. This approach places the emphasis where we believe it should be:

- ⁖ on teacher observation,
- ⁖ teaching to maximise current competencies,
- ⁖ and enhancing performance,

rather than on a child 'passing' and 'failing'.

This is the third edition of the *Record of Oral Language*. Since the first edition was published by the New Zealand Primary Teachers Institute in 1976 it has been used in different ways in New Zealand, South Australia, Queensland, USA, Liverpool, Glasgow and Edinburgh. When teachers from Reading Recovery programmes in any country seek to establish the quality of match between a child's score on this assessment and the texts in the books he is being asked to read, Record of Oral Language has proved useful in planning early literacy interventions.

Minor alterations to one or two words have been necessary for this assessment to be used in different English-speaking countries without losing its measurement qualities. Because the items have been carefully assessed by the appropriate statistical techniques used in standardised tests it has been clearly established that the sequence of item difficulty is surprisingly stable across very different groups of children. Research studies have shown that this assessment of oral language discriminates well among children in the United States who are five to seven years of age and have English as a mother tongue (Day and Day, 1978). It was also found to be sensitive to the assessment of changes in the language control for Fijian children who were learning English as a second language (Elley, 1991).

Groups of teachers working on professional or curriculum development projects have been able to use the assessment as a quick test for evaluating new language teaching programmes. The techniques have been useful in New Zealand for training professionals in how to observe and monitor changes in the language learning of non-English-speaking children, after they have had an introductory period in English language classes.

Using the R O L

Record of Oral Language assists teachers to:

‡ observe aspects of a child's control over oral language utterances, and

‡ assess a child's ability to handle selected grammatical structures.

There are two ways to gather evidence of change in sentence construction:

‡ Always use the Levels Sentences arranged in three levels of difficulty. (There are two examples of each type of sentence.)

‡ Select some Diagnostic Sentences if you need a more comprehensive exploration of a child's control of particular types of sentence. (Knowing something about the difficulty level of an item comes in handy when teachers are planning sequences of language instruction.)

These two ways may be used:

‡ to objectively observe/record a child's control of particular grammatical structures,

‡ to group children for specific teaching,

‡ to guide a teacher's own use of grammatical structures with certain children,

‡ or to assist a teacher to develop a child's control over some aspects of language in a systematic way.

Introduction

Why the concern about oral language?

Proficiency in oral language has long been considered important by teachers for self-expression and for communicating ideas. Morning talks, news and discussion sessions are familiar ways of encouraging children to reflect on their experience and to share their experience with others.

Educational psychologists like Jerome S. Bruner (1966) stressed proficiency in oral language because they regard it as a vital tool for thought. They would claim that without a fluent and structured oral language, children will find it very difficult to think abstractly and symbolically. That initial language, the basis of the child's thought, will be his first language whatever language that is.

Teachers also give particular attention to oral language in circumstances where the language or dialect a child uses in his home is different from the one the teacher uses in the classroom. It is usually considered to be important, both socially and educationally, for children to have an opportunity to learn more about their own language when their mother tongue is different from English. To this end, teachers need to know something of the different languages and different cultures of special groups of children.

However, teachers I work with are responsible for encouraging children to improve their skills in the use of the English language. Teachers therefore need to know something about the structure of the English language and how this structure is acquired by young children. This is as important as knowing about the different languages and cultures of the children they are teaching.

To date teachers have not had many procedures to help them to make objective assessments of how oral language changes over time. Nor have they been able to make objective appraisal of the oral language of different children. Any assessments that have been made rely heavily on teacher perception and judgement of rather gross qualities like 'style of delivery' or 'fluency', or alternatively, on tests of articulation and word knowledge.

A survey conducted in Auckland (Eillebrecht, 1971) asked teachers what they considered to be their greatest needs in teaching language. A simple method of testing children's levels of language performance was the second most popular request in a list of 14 expressed needs.

The Record of Oral Language was developed in response to that need. However, it is not designed as a test in the usual sense of the word. It was not intended merely to collect data (or scores) about change or to indicate the quality of instruction. It can be used in those ways but it was intended to be used for something much more important. It provides teachers with an instrument which they can use to adjust their teaching in a variety of ways.

❖ Using a sentence repetition method with five- and six-year-old children the R O L uncovers which sentence structures of English each young child has mastered. They were derived from research studies such as those of Graham (1968), Menyuk (1969) and Clay (1971). The teacher can record the most advanced structural level of oral language which a child might listen to with full understanding.

❖ By using these procedures a teacher can observe what developments have taken place in a child's control of some language structures from one time to another.

❖ The teacher might use the Record of Oral Language to assess change in oral language resulting from a special oral language programme, or simply from a child being in an environment where English is spoken.

❖ Results from use of the record could also provide a basis for selection of children whose language development requires special attention.

Why use sentence repetition to measure oral language?

One way to find out how much of the structure of adult speech a child has learned is to ask him to listen to a sentence and to repeat it. By having a child repeat sentences which represent a range of different syntactic structures in English a teacher can learn as much in a relatively short time about his control of those structures as would be learned from listening to the child's spontaneous speech over a much longer period.

There is growing evidence that it is very difficult for a teacher to assess a child's language control in a satisfactory manner on the basis of unstructured classroom observation alone. With time-consuming recording and analysis of large samples of a child's speech it is possible to describe the structures the child can produce. But research has shown that when we analyse a child's attempts to repeat a carefully constructed set of sentences we discover also those grammatical structures which he may be just beginning to understand but may not yet use in normal speech. Hence a child's ability to repeat sentences can give a more generous assessment of his ability to handle grammatical structure than is given by the language he himself produces.

Valuable information about a child's oral language can also be gathered from observing what he does with a sentence when asked to repeat one that is too difficult. The sentence repetition techniques are not used merely to record the items a child gets right or wrong.

❖ He may simply omit phrases, words or parts of words.

❖ He may substitute phrases, words or parts of words.

❖ He may expand the sentence by adding phrases or words.

❖ He may transpose some parts of a sentence.

An analysis of the responses a child gives to a set of sentences carefully ordered for difficulty yields a detailed description of his control over oral language. When a child fails, he usually repeats the difficult sentence in a way which indicates the structures over which he does have control.

By using the R O L sentences and making a precise recording on paper of children's attempts at repetition, a teacher has an objective means of describing changes in children's oral language.

Why does the R O L emphasise structure in language?

In everyday language, to paraphrase Lewis Carroll, we generally say what we mean and mean what we say. What we say (meaning) and how we say it (structure) are not always clearly distinguished. How to say things is patterned or structured by rules. These rules make what is said comprehensible. We may acquire the ability to use rules of structure before, or without, being aware of what they are.

A child who says 'I goed to town yesterday' appears to be applying a simple rule he has deduced from listening to others: namely if you mean something happened in the past, you add '-ed' to the simple form of the verb. The English language is more complicated than that, but despite such irregularities the structure of the language can provide information concerning the meaning of sentences.

If you heard a child say:

> There's the man what I saw at the shops yesterday,

it possibly represents considerable progress in language development over an earlier statement made by the child:

> See that man there. I saw him at the shops yesterday.

A child who says 'There's the man what I saw at the shops yesterday' is probably developing skill in using relative clauses; one can hardly expect him to learn when to use relative pronouns, and when not to use them, all at once. An attempt to correct this usage could well be interpreted by the child as a criticism of his experimental sentence. He could give up trying to change! Any setback in a child's efforts to develop his oral expression could well curtail his interest in understanding the complex things you say to him.

It is possible for competent adult readers to learn something from a sentence as apparently nonsensical as:

> A brom tribbed and wraggled the shoudy fline.

We can assume that a 'brom' did some 'tribbing' and 'wraggling' and that the 'brom' did it to 'the shoudy fline'. However, when the same words are rearranged as 'shoudy and tribbed brom fline a wraggled the', the structure does not provide the same clues to meaning.

Structure entails the classification of words or symbols into groups of different syntactic classes. Consider the following sentences.

John and Jane felt tired and angry with each other.
John and Jane felt tired and fought with each other.

By removing the words 'tired and' from the first sentence, an acceptable sentence remains:

John and Jane felt angry with each other.

However, removing the same words from the second sentence leaves only a nonsense sentence:

John and Jane felt fought with each other.

The two sentences differ in structure because 'angry' and 'fought' belong to quite different syntactic classes.

Structure can also be thought of as the way in which the meaning of a sentence is (in part) conveyed by the order of its components. In language the position and order of items play a considerable part in determining meaning. Note the effect of shifting 'not' in this pair of sentences.

Not all those children were given a turn.
All those children were not given a turn.

And compare these two sentences.

John hit Bill.
Bill hit John.

In the sentence:

The doctor gave the mother her baby.

the order of words tells us that it is the doctor that does the giving, the baby that is given, and the mother who gets what is given.

The manner in which words function is another way in which structure affects the meaning of sentences. These two sentences may appear to have the same structure.

I promised my mother to sweep the drive.
I told my mother to sweep the drive.

'Promised' and 'told' belong to the same class (verbs). However, those verbs have different functions; the first implies that 'I' will sweep the drive and the second that 'my mother' will sweep the drive.

If the average speaker did not have a reasonable knowledge of the basic rules of structure, communication would be difficult if not impossible. All speakers make their sentences fit with certain basic rules concerning the order of items, classes of items and combinations of classes. Nobody with a good grasp of English is in any doubt as to who does the shooting and who gets shot in:

> Bill shot John.

They would not omit 'that' from the following sentence:

> There's the man that gave the fruit to me.

They would know that it was optional in the following sentence:

> There's the man that I gave the fruit to.

The rule governing whether you can leave the 'that' out or not requires the same basic knowledge as is involved in knowing who did the shooting in 'Bill shot John'.

The procedures described in this manual are intended to help teachers to identify the extent of a child's knowledge of basic grammatical structures. To achieve this aim it is important for teachers to recognise steps in the acquisition of language skills so they may assist the process of development from simple forms to more complex ones. A young child is unlikely to understand the fine points of the English language until he has mastered the more common structures.

As a general rule children will use simple structures correctly, then attempt a more complex construction, then get close to correct use of the new syntax, before they get control over it. Observers must expect to see these cycles of change.

1 Administration of the Observation Task

Instructions for giving the Levels Sentences

The Levels Sentences can be used in a number of different ways. Teachers will develop ways of applying the Record of Oral Language and its findings to suit the needs of their particular class or school. The scalability of the Levels Sentences and their difficulty levels enables this assessment procedure to be adopted with confidence (see pages 48–50).

The observer/teacher reads each sentence aloud, as she talks normally to the child and he attempts to repeat it. Record exactly what the child says, immediately, on the record sheet for subsequent analysis.

On the line beneath each sentence on the record form:

1. Tick each word correctly repeated, and

2. Write in *every* deviation from the original sentence (even 'is' for ''s').

Examples: Level 2

Omission	That big dog over there is going to be my brother's. ✓ ✓ ✓ ✓ ✓ ✓ - - - ✓ ✓	A
Substitution *Omission*	The bird flew to the top of the tree. ✓ ✓ ✓ up - - - - -	C
Transposition *Substitution* *Omission*	For his birthday Mary gave him a truck. ✓ Mary's ✓ he ✓ ✓ - trucks.	D
Substitution *Addition*	Can you see what is climbing up the wall? ✓ ✓ ✓ that thing ✓ ✓ ✓ ✓ ✓ ?	E
Contraction *Addition* *Substitution*	There is my baby riding in his pushchair. ✓ 's a little ✓ ✓ ✓ her pram.	F

Note: The sentence is scored as correct only if it has been repeated *exactly*.

The child's response is scored as correct only if the sentence has been repeated exactly as presented. Each correctly repeated sentence is given a score of one point.

Accurate recording requires very careful listening. A common error is to predict that the child will give a correct response and assume that is what one heard. Tape recording of practice administrations provides a check on accuracy.

The R O L presents all the sentences from each level on a separate page. To reduce administration time, teachers should begin with Level 2 as this is the best starting point for most five-year-old children. However, it is open to the teacher to decide whether children who experience considerable difficulty should begin with Level 1 sentences. In exceptional circumstances where it is apparent that a child is not able to cope with the increasing difficulty of the sentences it is permissible to stop after three failures.

If a child is successful at repeating all the sentences at Level 2 he can be credited with passing all Level 1 sentences. If a child has difficulty with Level 2 sentences then he should be given those at Level 1.

Though it is permissible to begin at Level 1 and proceed to Level 2 and Level 3, the administration of the test is shortened by adopting the administration procedure summarised in the diagram on page 17.

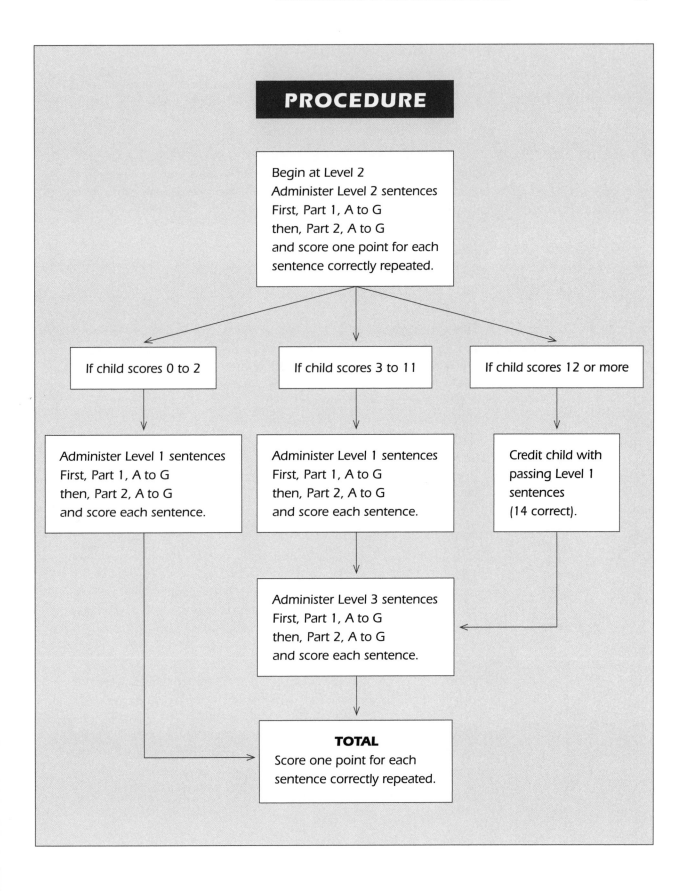

PROCEDURE

Begin at Level 2
Administer Level 2 sentences
First, Part 1, A to G
then, Part 2, A to G
and score one point for each
sentence correctly repeated.

| If child scores 0 to 2 | If child scores 3 to 11 | If child scores 12 or more |

Administer Level 1 sentences
First, Part 1, A to G
then, Part 2, A to G
and score each sentence.

Administer Level 1 sentences
First, Part 1, A to G
then, Part 2, A to G
and score each sentence.

Credit child with
passing Level 1
sentences
(14 correct).

Administer Level 3 sentences
First, Part 1, A to G
then, Part 2, A to G
and score each sentence.

TOTAL
Score one point for each
sentence correctly repeated.

Administration procedure

1. The record should be administered in a quiet place. Everything depends on the child being able *to hear your sentences clearly.* It is necessary that the sentences be presented out of the hearing of children who are to be assessed later.

2. Before beginning the administration, spend a few moments establishing rapport with the child. This can be done while you enter some information on the Record Form:

   Child's Name
   Class
   School
   Child's Date of Birth (obtain from school register)
   Date of Record
   Name of Recorder.

3. Begin by using this simple familiarisation procedure. Say: '*I would like you to say some sentences for me. Here is the first one.*
       Say — Tom is running to school.
       Good. Now say — I want Bill to come.
       Good. Now say — What is the time?
       Now let's try these.'

   If necessary, teachers can vary the instructions slightly to make sure that children understand what is required of them.

4. Throughout the administration of the sentences, make sure that you have the child's attention before presenting a new sentence. If the child's attention has wandered, wait until you have regained it before carrying on with further sentences. The child encounters two examples of each sentence type at each level. This is to ensure that failure on any one sentence due to momentary lapse of attention will not necessarily result in the child failing both sentences of that type.

5. The phrasing, or grouping of words, has been indicated by italics, but the sentences should be spoken clearly with natural intonation and pace.

It is permissible for schools or researchers to make copies of the Levels Sentences and Diagnostic Sentences for their own use. These should be set out in the same manner as in this book. It is essential that the sentences are copied with two types of print so that the items are administered with the correct phrasing.

Class: .... School: ....

Date of Birth: .... Date: ....

Child's Name: ....

Age: ....

Recorder: ....

The Levels Sentences

Level 2 Part 1.

Type

A *That big dog over there is going to be my brother's.* ☐

B *The boy by the pond was sailing his boat.* ☐

C *The bird flew to the top of the tree.* ☐

D *For his birthday Mary gave him a truck.* ☐

E *Can you see what is climbing up the wall?* ☐

F *Here comes a big elephant* with children sitting on his back. ☐

G *My brother turned the television up very loud.* ☐

Level 2 Part 2.

Type

A *That old truck in there* used to be *my father's.* ☐

B *The cat from next door was chasing a bird.* ☐

C *The dog ran through* the hole in the fence. ☐

D *For the holidays* Grandpa bought us a ball. ☐

E *The boy saw what* the man was doing *to the car.* ☐

F *There is my baby* riding in his pushchair. ☐

G *The girl threw her book* right across the room. ☐

Total for Level 2 [   ] /14

If the score is 12 or more, enter 14 on the next page for Level 1.

Level 1 Part 1.

Type

A *My brother's knees are dirty.*

B *Baby is drinking some milk.*

C *Sally is staying at home.*

D *John is buying me a boat.*

E *I know he's in there.*

F There's another fire engine.

G *She's driving her car quickly.*

Level 1 Part 2.

Type

A *The car's radio was stolen.*

B *Sally is riding her bike.*

C *Mary is going to town.*

D *Mary is giving me a book.*

E *I guess we're lost.*

F Here are some more fish.

G *He's playing that music very loud.*

Total for Level 1 ___/14

Level 3 Part 1.

Type

☐ **A** Be as quiet as you can when your father's asleep.

☐ **B** My aunt and uncle want to start building a new house.

☐ **C** The two cars drove along the road for a long time.

☐ **D** The baker sold my father some hot pies.

☐ **E** The girl saw who her mother was giving the cakes to.

☐ **F** They are the books that you were reading at my place.

☐ **G** My mother usually puts the cat out of the house at night.

Level 3 Part 2.

Type

☐ **A** Be very careful swimming when there's a big wave.

☐ **B** That dog and the one next door like to chase big cars.

☐ **C** All the children talked loudly to each other at the table.

☐ **D** The new teacher read our class a scary story.

☐ **E** The teacher knows how much wood we will need for the house.

☐ **F** There goes the fireman who put out the fire in the building.

☐ **G** My brother often puts some bread outside for the birds.

/14	Total for Level 3
/14	Level 1
/14	Level 2
/42	Grand Total

To select children for special help

For children in their first year of school the class teacher would probably want to give children in the lowest-scoring third of her class some extra time and some extra enriching activities in oral language, as well as the usual curriculum (not instead of it).

Although it will take time to administer the R O L to the whole class it is unwise for teachers to rely on the evidence of their unstructured observations or their intuitive feelings when deciding which children are in the lowest third of the class. If a teacher knows where each of her new entrants is on the R O L Levels Sentences, she can think of children as falling into three groups:

- those with high competence who bring rich language to the new tasks of reading and writing;
- those who have average skills and will need attention to make sure their oral language skills increase to cope as the school curriculum increases in difficulty;
- and thirdly, the group who need extra time and more conversations, and more enriching activities in oral language delivered concurrently with the reading and writing programmes of the classroom.

In general, children scoring below 13 will have acquired only a limited control over the structures of oral English. (The children will be more than one standard deviation below the average score for our normative sample.) They will be likely to have difficulty in following all but the simplest form of instructions given by the teacher and in following a story for their age group read to the class by the teacher. These children should be considered for special attention in oral language development. Children with a hearing loss may have low R O L performance.

The results invite teachers to ask questions

1. First, find the types and levels of sentences that a particular child can produce. (These are sentences he produces without a model to guide him.)

2. Make a list of activities for which that level of sentence structure would be okay. Does the class programme give the child opportunities to use this level of sentence-making successfully?

3. Think of two or three situations in the classroom where the person speaking to this child would only be using more difficult structures. In those situations does this child try to respond? With what success?

4. Look at an average sentence in this child's writing. Does he write sentences like the ones he passed on the test? Or are they shorter and less complex than his speech?

5. With whom should this child be talking if he is to have an enriching opportunity to learn more about the language in conversation? When does he try to lift the level of his spoken sentences? (Hint: when retelling a story he has heard several times or when he recites a rhyme he has learned.)

6. Think of the reading you expect this child to do. Are the books

   below,
   a fair match,
   or above his level of sentence construction?

7. Can he use his current knowledge of sentence construction for the reading tasks you give him?

   If you decide that the sentence construction is too complex for him, ask yourself whether you are introducing the new book as a challenge to his sentence construction. Is it an appropriate challenge? Are you providing an appropriate level of support? Or are you expecting him to reach a higher level of sentence organisation without giving him your support? To support the child, provide the model. Say the sentence, or structure, before he is expected to read it.

Instructions for using the Diagnostic Sentences

The Levels Sentences were all declarative sentences — they made simple statements. Those simple statements can be turned into questions and negatives. They can have phrases and clauses added to increase their complexity. Yet our research has shown that even the most complex sentences in these lists are still within the spoken language ability of the higher achievers in the age group.

The Diagnostic Sentences are variations of the simple sentence types. A teacher with a good ear for language may be able to decide that a particular child has trouble with formulating questions, or with negative statements, or *that he does not know how to fit more information into a simple sentence.*

When the teacher knows where the child begins to fail on the Levels Sentences, she can do a little more exploring. Hearing the child use a queer form of question, she could explore this a little more systematically by giving him the diagnostic questions to repeat. She presents these extra items in the same manner as the Levels Sentences. All she has to do is record immediately exactly what the child says so she can compare performances across all her records later.

The Diagnostic sentence types were generated from the same sentence types that are in the Levels task. They have been changed (or transformed) into

imperative sentences (the easiest sentence form for young children)
questions
negative sentences

or changed by adding

pre-posed phrases
relative clauses and
adverbial clauses.

A child may repeat a Levels sentence correctly but fail on its Diagnostic versions. Or there may be a Diagnostic Sentence which he repeats correctly although he was not successful with the Levels Sentence. One does not predict the other! The Diagnostic Sentences do not fit into the levels of difficulty for the Levels task. Some children find most of the items hard. And the Diagnostic Sentences do not exhaust the variations that can occur in the language.

Within each group (imperatives, negatives, and so on) the Diagnostic Sentences are arranged in the order of difficulty experienced by the children in our main study. There is a steep gradient of difficulty within each group.

Any new type of sentence a child attempts is a step forward, even if it is only half correct.

Imperatives — I

Item

1 *Come and watch him climbing the tree.* ☐

2 *Go and play with your brother in the garden for a while.* ☐

3 *Go to the doctor's with your sister now!* ☐

4 *Hang John's coat on the hook for him.* ☐

5 *Hurry and get the children a few crayons.* ☐

Imperatives — II

Item

6 *Fix my shirt and pants please.* ☐

7 *Go and look for your bag in the kitchen after dinner.* ☐

8 *Ask for some apples at the shop, then.* ☐

9 *Shine the torch on the steps for the visitor.* ☐

10 *Run and find the milkman two more bottles.* ☐

Questions — II

Item

21 *Are you lending him your pencil?*

22 *Did the teacher see the boy chasing me?*

23 *They've gone, haven't they?*

24 *Are we going to Grandma's for lunch tomorrow?*

25 *What did the boy want to make for his brother?*

26 *Is the cup in your hand full or empty?*

27 *Most boys and girls like swimming, don't they?*

28 *Did you see the policeman last night chasing robbers on his bike?*

29 *How much of the wood will we need to build a boat?*

30 *Did any of the children catch the lollies he threw?*

Questions — I

Item

11 *Are you selling him your bike?*

12 *Did you watch the man lighting the fire?*

13 *He won't lose my puppy dog, will he?*

14 *Can I play with Jane at her house now?*

15 *Where did the lady try to hide her money?*

16 *Is the truck by the gate red or green?*

17 *The old man isn't very good at swimming, is he?*

18 *Can the driver see the cars all right in the dark?*

19 *What kind of fruit will we buy to make some jam?*

20 *Did any of the birds eat the bread you fed them?*

Negatives — II

Item

☐ 39 *Some people can't drink strong tea.*

☐ 40 *Peter's father wouldn't get him a school bag.*

☐ 41 *Don't be so careless with that sharp knife.*

☐ 42 *Peter's father isn't home from work yet.*

☐ 43 *The boy didn't want to climb very high up the ladder.*

☐ 44 *He didn't move his car far enough off the road.*

☐ 45 *(No satisfactory item)*

☐ 46 *The policeman in the car isn't really your father, is he?*

Negatives — I

Item

☐ 31 *Most cows can't eat short grass.*

☐ 32 *Mary's teacher didn't give her a tick.*

☐ 33 *Don't be so nasty to your little brother.*

☐ 34 *Jason's book isn't in his bag any more.*

☐ 35 *The bird can't fly very far in the rain.*

☐ 36 *The girl didn't find any milk in the fridge for the baby.*

☐ 37 *The ladies didn't want to stay outside in the rain.*

☐ 38 *The car over there isn't really your brother's, is it?*

Phrases — II

Item

☐ 54 *In a minute* we'll play *in the sandpit.*

☐ 55 *On television* the children watched *Play School.*

☐ 56 *The boys let ten balls* roll slowly down the hill.

☐ 57 *This year* we're going to a farm *for the holidays.*

☐ 58 *On Saturday* Aunty brought us *a box of chocolates.*

☐ 59 *On the way to school* we watched some men *digging a hole in the road.*

☐ 60 *Under the car* there were two black cats.

Phrases — I

Item

☐ 47 *On Saturday* the boy is going *to the circus.*

☐ 48 *At the hospital* the nurses saw *the doctor.*

☐ 49 *The lady stopped playing the piano* to listen to the children.

☐ 50 *In a minute* we'll go and look for him *in the garden.*

☐ 51 *Last weekend* his father made him *a sailing boat.*

☐ 52 *On Monday* John took his puppy *to school with him.*

☐ 53 *In the nest* there were three baby birds.

Clauses — II

Item

□ **72** *Jane's at home* because it's a holiday.

□ **73** *He thanked me very much* when I gave him the ball.

□ **74** *The girl who(m) we passed* was wearing boots.

□ **75** *Bill showed me the bike* you sent him.

□ **76** *When the room is tidy* we will be ready for our story.

□ **77** *I asked John for the ball* I threw to him.

□ **78** *If the stone has broken the window* my father will make me fix it.

□ **79** *Bill's looking for a bike* that goes very fast.

□ **80** *When my friends came to my place* we played outside all afternoon.

□ **81** *When the man put the box on the table* he knocked a cup on the floor.

□ **82** *That is the book* that was on the table.

Clauses — I

Item

□ **61** *John's in bed* because he's been sick.

□ **62** *I threw him the ball* because he asked me to.

□ **63** *The man who(m) I met* was mowing the lawn.

□ **64** *I gave Linda the book* she showed me.

□ **65** *If his father isn't home* the boy will be sad.

□ **66** *I want some bread for the bird* I found outside.

□ **67** *After he had his breakfast* the boy brushed his teeth.

□ **68** *Jane's playing with the girl* who lives next door.

□ **69** *If the cat climbs on the roof* the birds will fly away again.

□ **70** *While you mind my bike for me* I'll take my bag inside.

□ **71** *This is the chocolate* that was in my bag.

When would I want to use the Diagnostic Sentences?

If, for example, I heard a child using a negative sentence in an unusual way I might decide to use *both* the Levels Sentences task plus the Diagnostic Sentences for negatives to explore this problem. That is:

- ÷ I would find out what types of simple sentences the child can and cannot control in the Levels Sentences.

- ÷ Then, turning to the Negative Sentences in the Diagnostic Sentences, I would check the child's ability to repeat Negatives I. For a double-check I could give the child a second chance on the parallel item types in Negatives II.

- ÷ After three failed items in any one list it is good practice to discontinue testing as further success is unlikely.

From this information I would make some judgements about the structures that were causing problems and about the content to use in remedial exercises.

But after I had decided on a plan of action to emphasise some aspect of language with this child I would discuss my plan and my reasons with a couple of colleagues. Why do this? It is because as users of a language we often 'cannot see the wood for the trees'!

2 Application

1. Provide a competent adult model

The most effective way of raising the level of a child's control over the structures of English is to provide him with many opportunities to hold a real conversation with a competent and flexible speaker of English. This competent speaker (usually an adult) should be able to:

- ÷ speak English fluently,
- ÷ get to know the child's particular interests and enthusiasms,
- ÷ get to know what particular words and expressions mean for particular children,
- ÷ share ideas and experiences with the child using sentences only a little more complex than the ones the child is using.

Assistance with this very important aspect of oral language development could be provided by teachers in training while working alongside a class teacher, or by voluntary helpers guided closely by the better-informed class teacher who did the testing. The critical qualification is being able to talk *with* a child. (Evaluate carefully the English language fluency of older children or speakers for whom English is not their mother tongue as mentors for this targeted group must create interactions designed to achieve maximum results in a minimum of individual time.)

2. Analyse the record

Study the child's responses to the Levels Sentences which he found difficult.

Do not make allowances for replies which give you the gist of the sentence but not the accurate repetition!

- ÷ Look for any patterning of errors.
- ÷ Try to establish what he does when he changes the sentence.
- ÷ Does he omit words, substitute words or expand the sentences?
- ÷ Do these changes occur with particular types of sentences?
- ÷ What could account for a particular kind of error?
- ÷ Is there a word or phrase in the sentence that he does not know?

⁘ Try out some sentences of your own that use the same structure but use different, more familiar words. This will help determine if the child's difficulty is due to vocabulary demands (i.e., word choice or meaning) that render the sentence more difficult than expected.

3.   Adjust the classroom language

Identify the types of sentences the child is able to repeat correctly, and use these to guide your selection of texts for this child when you need him to be a successful reader or writer. Then teach him new structures by using slight changes in structure in one or two sentence types, to extend his control over producing sentences.

4.   Begin at the level of sentences the child can handle

Start by talking about experiences this child wants to talk about. These provide the opportunities to encourage the development of the child's control of sentence patterns. If you decide to attend to more complex structure in sentences, then the child should begin with sentence types that he can repeat without error.

The basis of any individual work is the provision of plenty of conversation with an adult using sentences at the level the child can easily control. There should be no urgency to hurry the child on to more difficult sentences. On the other hand the programme must have the spontaneity and naturalness of conversation. *Repetitive exercises will not shift the child's control of structure.*

The goal is to become more flexible and to try alternative ways of putting ideas together.

5.   Select sentences for special attention

Locate a sentence type in the Levels or Diagnostic Sentences that you expect the child to repeat successfully. Make up a sentence of parallel structure.

> *The R O L sentences themselves must not be used as practice items.*
> *Make up sentences of similar structure.*

Use this sentence structure in your conversation. If, for example, a child has difficulty with a Level 2 form then try him with Level 1 prior to eventually moving back to Level 2. If he is comfortable with a Level 2 form then try him with a Level 3 example. Do not move up the level of difficulty too soon!

Think about the *two* gradients of difficulty in the Levels Sentences.

⁘ The easier ones are placed earlier in each group of Levels Sentences. Thus Type A sentences are generally easier than Type B, and Type F are easier than Type G.

✛ The second gradient of difficulty is *within each sentence type*. In general. Level 1 examples of sentence types are easier than Level 2 sentences. A child who is successful on sentence Types A, B and C at Level 1 might progress towards understanding more elaborate examples like those of similar type which are illustrated by Level 2 sentences of A, B and C type.

6. Generating practice sentences

Teachers can use the descriptions on pages 39–41 as a guide for practising how to make up sentences of the required type. It may help teachers to simplify or increase complexity of a sentence type to make up a sentence and then to compare it with a similar sentence type on Levels 1, 2 and 3. How hard was your sentence? (See pages 42–44.)

As an example, new Type B sentences could be written by substituting appropriately in the item sentences.

		Subject	**Verb**	**Direct Object**
Level 1	Item:	Baby	is drinking	some milk.
	Exercise:	Mary	is waving	a flag.
Level 2	Item:	The boy by the pond	was sailing	his boat.
	Exercise:	The girl with the hat	was bouncing	her ball.
Level 3	Item:	My aunt and uncle	want to start building	a new house.
	Exercise:	The doctor and his wife	need to lose	some weight.

Substitutions of this kind will not automatically generate sentences of suitable difficulty. The factors which influence difficulty are very complex. However, as teachers gain experience in writing sentences of a given type, and especially of using those sentences with children, they should find the writing easier. It should also become more likely that the sentences written are of appropriate difficulty.

7. Introduce more difficult sentences in a systematic manner

Problems will be created for the child if teachers confront the child with *too many* new features simultaneously.

This can occur when a teacher does not consider the sentences that the child is currently using. Children can handle imperative sentences and short declarative sentences with relative ease. Therefore, in the early stages of a language programme it is wise for the teacher to limit the number of words, the number of phrases, the number of clauses, and the number of embellishments that are used. Encourage flexibility in how pupils use a variety of simple structures as a first step.

Introduce a new feature (for example, the indirect object) into a simple sentence of familiar structures. *The new feature should be the only difficulty.*

- ❖ If the familiar structure is 'John is buying a boat', then a new feature to be introduced might be 'John is buying a boat for me', followed a little later by 'John is buying me a boat'.
- ❖ Use rhythm, intonation and meaning to direct attention to the new feature.

In the Diagnostic section there are systematic variations on the simple statement forms used in the Levels Sentences. Moreover, it is usual to find the following.

- ❖ Imperative sentences are easy.
- ❖ Questions are relatively easy.
- ❖ Negative sentences are fairly difficult.
- ❖ Extra phrases in front lengthen and complicate a sentence.
- ❖ Adverbial clauses further increase the difficulty.
- ❖ Relative clauses are difficult to fit into a sentence.

The Diagnostic Sentences provide one way of varying complexity. Appropriate selections must be made to suit the particular needs of a child.

8. Check on progress

Use the Levels Sentences to check on a child's progress over time.

The Record of Oral Language may be administered at intervals of six months.

If, for research or monitoring reasons, a teacher needed to check progress at three-month intervals, then using Part 1 only on the first occasion and Part 2 only on the second occasion (for Levels or Diagnostic Sentences) could be considered. (*Caution:* This reduces the reliability of the observation.)

- ❖ Teachers may want to discover how many more structures the child can handle after he has spent some time in a special oral language programme.
- ❖ Teachers may want to check, after the child has spent some time in the classroom programme, whether he is making any noticeable progress.

3 Speakers of other dialects or other languages

Other dialects

If you hear a child from an English-speaking home say

> Her b'aint a-calling we: us don't belong-a she.

he is probably speaking the language heard in his home. The school is expected to help the child to learn to read books which might say

> She isn't calling us: we don't belong to her.

Both statements are from rule-guided oral language, and every day the child comes from and returns to a home where the first set of rules is used in everyday conversation.

After many years of discussion there is a consensus among authorities that, because the child has already learned those rules and needs to use them in his community, we cannot regard the use of the dialect to be wrong. What we need to do is to teach the child another way of saying the same thing (that is to teach him another set of rules for a second dialect). We must help him to understand when to use each dialect. For example, we can say 'In school books the author has written that message in another way.'

Children are flexible and they are good language learners. They can learn to use one dialect in one setting and a different dialect in another setting. One of the teacher's tasks is to encourage the child to increase his ability to adjust his language to his task or setting.

Other languages

A school entrant who already speaks another language may have a bigger problem. He will have a set of rules which works well in his first language and which are often not applicable when he speaks English. Then in addition, he may well have learned some English in his home or community that is spoken by an adult who does not speak English very well. So the student we are dealing with may already have either one or two confusing sets of rules for 'making sentences'.

That child will depend on a teacher's conversations with him if he is to hear and use a different set of rules. Learning new rules will take time. It involves more complex learning than merely learning new words. It takes a two-year-old child three to five years to do this basic language learning.

That child will begin simply, and slowly in much the same way as a younger child learns English as his mother tongue. But he is older and if he is encouraged to use simple structures which are useful and used frequently, he could move quite rapidly through a sequence of learning how to construct English sentences.

His teacher must be sharply vigilant and offer maximum help when anything in the talk of either the child or the teacher is 'irregular rather than regular', or is infrequently used, or is out of the ordinary.

This child cannot work out what he should say from some hunch about the rule system like first-language children can. Some expert speaker of the language must let him 'hear' the irregular example several times and in different contexts before he will be tempted to try it. Authors of children's books often include unusual language features which children like to repeat!

Other cultures

Record of Oral Language has been used in Scotland and Liverpool where the English spoken is different in some ways from New Zealand English, with bilingual Chinese, Dutch and Samoan children in New Zealand, and with monolingual English-speaking children. It was used with a large sample of Maori children in New Zealand who were tested and found to be monolingual in English, and with children who had language difficulties and were referred for speech therapy.

In all these widely different samples the item statistics varied very little. Our results strongly support the conclusion that the sequence of item difficulty which was obtained for the R O L sentences (see pages 46–47) do not vary much for any of the groups tested.

Different language groups may score at different levels on the ROL but their control over the structures used in English sentences seems to be learned in much the same order (give or take some minor exceptions). The learners seem to travel much the same path but at a slower pace.

4   A final word

Children who are learning to speak English catch on to the rules,

- ✛ first by grasping the easy structures,
- ✛ then those of medium difficulty,
- ✛ and finally those of greater difficulty which include those of infrequent or irregular usage.

Children master the complexity of English without the benefit of formal tuition in how to speak. In the face of such fantastic skill and the complex nature of language learning, it would be presumptuous for anyone to assume that the R O L sentences can serve as a sufficient basis for devising a teaching sequence on its own.

Obviously vocabulary must be accumulated, and the phonemic basis of the new language is of vital importance. But teaching only sounds, letters and words will fall far short of what the language learner needs. How to construct sentences so that they will carry messages is an essential component of speaking, writing and reading.

However, it is hoped that using the R O L sentences from time to time will provide teachers of young children with awareness of features which will allow a learner to master a wide range of structural knowledge about English sentences. R O L sentences should help teachers to develop more powerful language programmes.

Teachers will be primarily concerned with fostering interest and spontaneity in oral language activities but hopefully using the R O L sentences from time to time will help them to see how recording and assessing changes in children's oral language can increase the effectiveness of their teaching for children who are not average or better in oral communication. Teachers who use the Record of Oral Language will be able to develop their own applications of the findings to suit their particular needs. And consultation among a group of colleagues is very helpful.

5 Technical appendices

This section is an optional extra intended more for researchers and programme developers than for classroom teachers.

1 Linguistic aspects: The development of the Levels and Diagnostic Sentences

In 1973 an initial pilot testing and a subsequent full-scale testing programme in Auckland schools examined five- to six-year olds' ability to repeat sentences. This research extended the previous work of Clay (1971). The Pilot Programme included particular variants of 10 different sentence types so that a total of 369 sentences (see page 44) were included in the initial list.

Detailed analyses of children's success at repeating these sentences led to a careful selection and ordering of 42 sentences which were shown to represent a gradient of difficulty from easy to difficult. The sentences selected were largely restricted to those of a simple statement (declarative) form. These sentences constitute the items of the Levels Sentences.

From the other variations of simple sentences (such as negative sentences and sentences with relative clauses) some additional sets of sentences were selected to construct the Diagnostic Sentences task. The Diagnostic Sentences can be used following the administration of the Levels Sentences if a more comprehensive exploration of a child's command of English is desirable.

The Levels Sentences are grouped on the basis of three levels of difficulty. Each level contains two examples of each sentence type and the seven different types are described in the following pages.

The sentence types used in the Levels Sentences

Type A: These sentences are composed of a noun phrase (the *subject*) followed by some form of the *verb 'to be'* and some other *simple statement.* They cannot have an object.

Examples:	Subject	Verb 'to be'	Simple Statement
Level 1	My brother's knees	are	dirty.
	The car's radio	was	stolen.
Level 2	That big dog over there	is going to be	my brother's.
	That old truck in there	used to be	my father's.
Level 3	(You)	Be	as quiet as you can when your father's asleep.
	(You)	Be	very careful swimming when there's a big wave.

Note: In Level 3 the imperative form has been used. In these two sentences a subject ('You') is implied.

Type B: These sentences are composed of a noun or noun phrase (the *subject*) followed by a *verb phrase,* followed by a noun phrase which is a *direct object.*

Examples:	Subject	Verb Phrase	Direct Object
Level 1	Baby	is drinking	some milk.
	Sally	is riding	her bike.
Level 2	The boy by the pond	was sailing	his boat.
	The cat from next door	was chasing	a bird.
Level 3	My aunt and uncle	want to start building	a new house.
	That dog and the one next door	like to chase	big cars.

Type C: These sentences are composed of a noun or noun phrase (the *subject)* followed by *a verb or verb phrase* followed by one of a variety of *additional constructions* which is not a direct object.

Examples:	Subject	Verb/Verb Phrase	Additional Construction
Level 1	Sally	is staying	at home.
	Mary	is going	to town.
Level 2	The bird	flew	to the top of the tree.
	The dog	ran	through the hole in the fence.
Level 3	The two cars	drove	along the road for a long time.
	All the children	talked	loudly to each other at the table.

Type D: These sentences are composed of a noun or noun phrase (the *subject)* followed by a *verb* or *verb phrase* followed by two noun phrases forming the *indirect* and the *direct objects.*

Examples:	Subject	Verb/Verb Phrase	Indirect Object	Direct Object
Level 1	John	is buying	me	a boat.
	Mary	is giving	me	a book.
Level 2	(For his birthday) Mary	gave	him	a truck.
	(For the holidays) Grandpa	bought	us	a ball.
Level 3	The baker	sold	my father	some hot pies.
	The new teacher	read	our class	a scary story.

Note: The Level 2 sentences contain a proposed noun phrase (in brackets) because this proved to be the best item in terms of statistical criteria for the difficulty sequence.

Type E: These sentences are composed of a noun phrase (the *subject)* followed by a *verb* followed by a *noun clause.*

Examples:	Subject	Verb	Noun Clause
Level 1	I	know	he's in there.
	I	guess	we're lost.
Level 2	Can you	see	what is climbing up the wall?
	The boy	saw	what the man was doing to the car.
Level 3	The girl	saw	who her mother was giving the cakes to.
	The teacher	knows	how much wood we will need for the house.

Note: In Level 2 the question form provided the best item in terms of statistical criteria for the difficulty sequence.

Type F: These sentences are composed of an *adverb* (for example 'here' or 'there') or a *relative pronoun* (for example 'this', 'that', 'these') followed by a *verb* (for example 'be', 'come', 'go') followed by the *subject* of the sentence.

Examples:	Adverb/ Relative Pronoun	Verb	Subject
Level 1	There	's	another fire engine.
	Here	are	some more fish.
Level 2	Here	comes	a big elephant with children sitting on his back.
	There	is	my baby riding in his pushchair.
Level 3	There	are	the books that you were reading at my place.
	There	goes	the fireman who put out the fire in the building.

Type G: These sentences are composed of a noun phrase(the *subject*), followed by a *verb* or *verb phrase*, followed by an *object*, followed by some *additional construction* (for example adverb or adverbial phrase).

Examples:	**Subject**	**Verb/ Verb Phrase**	**Object**	**Additional Construction**
Level 1	She	's driving	her car	quickly.
	He	's playing	that music	very loud.
Level 2	My brother	turned	the television	(up) very loud.
	The girl	threw	her book	right across the room.
Level 3	My mother	usually puts	the cat	out of the house at night.
	My brother	often puts	some bread	outside for the birds.

The basic structures used in the Levels Sentences are summmarised in the following table.

Type A	Nbe+	Bill	was		asleep.
Type B	NVN	Bill	saw	John.	
Type C	NV+	Bill	went		to town.
Type D	NVNN	Bill	sent	John/a book.	
Type E	NVN clause	Bill	knows	what he wants.	
Type F	Here/There	Here	are	some more fish.	
Type G	NVN+	Bill	sent	John	to town.

This is a very simplified way of recording a phrase structure description of the sentence types of English. N stands for a noun or noun phrase, V for all parts of the verb, and the plus sign (+) is used for a variety of structures that can occur in that position. The analysis can be aligned with that used in Scott, Bowley, Brockett, Brown and Goddard (1968). More discussion of the sentences' variants could be found in any of the printings of the 1983 edition (Clay, Gill, Glynn, McNaughton, Salmon). The relationship of R O L's simplified description of sentence structures to the more rigorous linguistic description is explained there.

The R O L sentences could not hope to cover exhaustively the great variety of structures found in English. They deal only with the structures that were within the ability and experience of the average child of five years.

The origin of the items

Examples of child utterances were compiled from the literature on language acquisition and from a pilot study. However as very few structures needed in the matrix were well represented, the majority of the items were made up using a frequency list of child vocabulary (Edwards and Gibbon, 1964) and an Australian research study of sentences used by five-year-old children (Harwood, 1959).

The linguistic difficulty of the items

No single linguistic criterion has been devised for predicting reliably the difficulty of sentences. A combination of factors was used in the creation of the item sentences. There are many factors which influence the difficulty of any sentence. An unusual word or ambiguity of meaning could easily cause an increase in difficulty greater than that produced by a change in grammatical structure or an increase in sentence length. The most reliable guide to difficulty is the nature of children's responses.

The following factors were used to control the difficulty of sentences in the R O L and should be borne in mind when creating new examples.

1. *Morpheme Counts* may not provide a reliable guide to the difficulty of encoding and decoding utterances. For example, in

   | *He is coming* | (4 morphemes) |
   | *I come* | (2 morphemes) |

   the first sentence has greater frequency in speech and is probably less difficult for the child to repeat than the shorter second one. Also, the problems introduced by affixes and by fused morphemes makes a measure of morpheme count very difficult to apply in a systematic way. However, an attempt was made to keep the morpheme count relatively consistent within each level. Where a sentence has a markedly different morpheme count from other sentences of that type or level it is because other factors have affected its difficulty to a greater extent.

2. *Phrase Count.* The number of phrases in a phrase structure description of the basic sentence must vary because that number is determined by the sentence type. For example, the imperatives necessarily do not have a subject phrase. Sometimes a phrase was added (for example as a qualifier of a nominal group). Nevertheless the difficulty level of a particular item could be increased by including additional phrases such as a qualifier of a nominal group. Sentence difficulty was varied by such additions.

3. *Difficult Features.* From research reports it was found that children of this age found the following features difficult:

❖ words not often used ('nurse');

❖ words of greater complexity ('shopkeeper');

❖ contracted forms;

❖ infrequently used tenses;

❖ irregular forms of verbs and nouns;

❖ complex verbal groups;

❖ coordinated groups;

❖ final rather than initial placement of adverbial phrases or clauses.

To achieve a progression from easy Level 1 examples of a sentence type to Level 2 or 3 examples, some of these difficult features were introduced.

4. *Number of Actors.* Equivalence was sought with respect to the number of actors appearing in paired sentences. Compare the following:

> May I play with Bill at his house?
> May I play with Bill at Jim's house?

In the second sentence, 'Jim's' introduces an extra person and thus an extra semantic element to handle.

5. *Ambiguities.* To avoid ambiguities in sentences with two or more actors when pronouns were used, the actors were differentiated by sex. Also, sentences were avoided where the syntax could be misinterpreted momentarily during decoding. Examples are:

> That lady teacher . . .
>   'teach' initially classed as a verb.
> The footballers
>   'ers' misinterpreted as 'is'.

6. *Syntactic Structure of Items.* It was the aim that each clause in a multiclause sentence should conform to the structure type. Certain exceptions were allowed in order to produce natural sentences.

   Nominal groups serving a syntactic function in two clauses were regarded as fulfilling the qualification for the basic clause type in each clause; the same consideration applied to relative pronouns.

7. *Semantic Acceptability.* The Australian and English word frequency lists used did not guarantee that the high frequency words used would be known to New Zealand children and the only other means of controlling for meaning was to have the sentences checked by two trained teachers of this age-group.

In summary: if the test items were intended to probe syntactic control then ideally, phonological, morphological, lexical and semantic aspects of the sentences should not increase the sentence difficulty. One approach would be to use only a limited list of words and morphemes. However, there is also the need to gain the child's cooperation and therefore the sentences should maintain a reasonable level of variety and naturalness. Thus, at the stage of item writing the difficulty of the items was manipulated by:

- using a detailed matrix of structures,
- counting morphemes,
- counting phrases,
- noting the difficulty of features,
- avoiding ambiguities,
- matching clause structures in multiclause sentences,
- keeping the meaning as simple as possible, and
- using high frequency words.

The construction of test items

For the pilot study 369 items were compiled and they represent cells in the following matrix of structures.

Transformations								
Type	Basic Structures	Declarative	Imperative	Yes-No Question	Negative	Proposed Phrase	Relative Clause	Adverbial Clause
A	Nbe+							
B	NVN							
C	NV+							
D	NVNN							
G	NVN+							

Supplementary sentence types in addition to those in the matrix were

Here be . . .
Wh- questions
Tag questions
Multi-predicated clauses
Noun clauses — two sets

Thus there were 35 structures in the matrix and six supplementary types giving a total of 41 sets. Each set had three levels of difficulty (123 subsets) and each subset contained three equivalent examples. This gave 369 items in all.

2 The development research

The pilot study

Sample

The selection of the actual items for the R O L necessitated the administration of the 369 items forming the item pool, to a random sample of children of the types for whom the instrument was intended. Thus, from a sampling frame of the 238 state and private schools of the Auckland metropolitan area, a random sample of approximately one tenth (24 schools) was selected. This was done with probability of selection being proportional to size, and with replacement. From each of these sample schools, a second stage random sample of 10 children was chosen. The sampling frame within each school was all those children who were between 5:0 and 6:0 years at testing.

Testing procedure

As 369 items were considered to be too many for any child to be given, a procedure was devised so that no child was given items unnecessarily. No easy items were given to a child who passed the items of average difficulty, and no difficult ones were given to children failing those of average difficulty.

It was necessary to decide on a consistent way of scoring some responses. An example of this is the use of 'is' or its shortened version (apostrophe 's'). Both versions may indicate that the child has control over the grammatical structure, but the statistics for the R O L have been calculated on the basis of the scoring method described, which is exact repetition. In a trial rescoring analysis allowing both full and contracted forms to be scored as correct, the difficulty level of the items changed only minimally.

The sequence of types and variants was designed not only so that items of a structure were separated from each other, but also so that easier forms were interspersed between more difficult ones. Further, similar structures were separated from one another.

Item analysis

For each item, the following statistics were calculated:

(i) the difficulty index;

(ii) a discrimination index, based on top and bottom 27 percent groups

(iii) the point biserial correlation between that item and the test as a whole.

Further, the sample was split at the median, and the statistics were recalculated separately for the top 50 percent and bottom 50 percent.

Selection of the items

The R O L was to have three levels of difficulty. Thus, the difficulty of an item, as demonstrated by the pilot study, was a core concern when its inclusion in the instrument was being considered. However, other criteria also had to be satisfied.

(i) The R O L had to be of practical use to teachers, and therefore its components had to be ones which separately and together were pertinent to the classroom situation.

(ii) The set of items to be selected for the R O L had to make linguistic sense. That is, there had to be a clear linguistic rationale for the item statistics of the items making up the R O L.

(iii) Each item had to satisfy certain statistical criteria:

    a) It had to be comparatively easy for children who turned out to be above the median on the final instrument and comparatively difficult for those below the median.

    b) It had to discriminate well among the children ranked at the top on the instrument and among those ranked at the bottom end.

    c) It had to measure the same underlying ability as the instrument as a whole measured.

    d) It had to have a difficulty appropriate for the sentence type and consistent with the other items at that level.

The Levels Sentences deliberately are selected at varying difficulty levels. The difficulty indices range from .15 to .89. There is no overlap in difficulty from level to level in the Field Trial data graphed on page 51.

An examination of the item statistics from the pilot study showed that it was indeed possible to construct a test with three levels of difficulty *and* satisfy all the above criteria. This was done by using the declarative form of the five basic sentence types, one of the noun clause structures, and the 'here be +' sentences to select a form other than the declarative in order to get satisfactory item statistics. Instead of the declarative form of NVNN structure in the middle difficulty set of items, the one actually used contains a pre-posed phrase.

> *For his birthday Kiri gave him a truck.*

Similarly, of the more difficult items, the declarative form of an Nbe+ item was not suitable according to the statistical criteria, and the imperative form

> *Be as quiet as you can when your father's asleep.*

was included.

It was possible to find two items of each structure at each difficulty level which satisfied the criteria. Thus, the core of the Levels Sentences consists of two examples of each of seven sentence types at each of three levels of difficulty. That is, 42 items constitute the Levels Sentences section of the Record of Oral Language.

There were, however, many other statistically sound items. These then formed the pool of items from which further selection resulted in the construction of the Diagnostic Sentences.

The main study

Sample

In order to test the instrument generated by the pilot study, and obtain valid item statistics on all 123 items of the test, it was necessary to sample randomly from the Auckland metropolitan schools again, this time using the information gained from the pilot study in regard to (i) mean school size, (ii) variation within schools, (iii) variation between schools, (iv) mean cost to visit a school for testing pupils, and (v) cost of testing a child. When these factors were weighted appropriately using an optimum allocation formula, it was found necessary to test three children from each of 131 schools.

As with the pilot study, the 238 state and private schools in the area constituted the sampling frame, and 131 of these were randomly selected, with probability of selection being proportional to size. Each school was returned to the sampling frame after selection. From each of the sample schools a second-stage random sample of three 5:0- to 6:0-year-olds was taken and tested.

Testing procedure

The testers visited one school each day. At the beginning of the school day they obtained their random sample of children who were between 5:0 and 6:0 years on that day, and then spent the rest of the day testing them. Each child was called back three or four times in order to have him complete all 123 items of the instrument.

The order of presentation of the items was as follows:

  (i) The Level 2 items

 (ii) The Level 1 items

(iii) The Level 3 items

(iv) The easiest Diagnostic items

 (v) The hardest Diagnostic items.

However, within each of the above sets, the sentences were sequenced in the same way as they had been in the pilot study. That is, (i) similar items were separated from one another; (ii) item pairs were separated maximally; and (iii) easier forms were interspersed between more difficult ones.

Item analysis

Using the whole sample, the same basic item analyses as for the pilot study were undertaken. The item statistics were as follows:

Levels Sentences — Item Statistics

Level 1, Part 1 items	A	B	C	D	E	F	G
Difficulty index	.74	.87	.89	.85	.86	.87	.68
Discrimination index	.46	.27	.21	.29	.26	.24	.49
Point biserial correlation	.51	.46	.38	.46	.37	.34	.47

Level 1, Part 2 items	A	B	C	D	E	F	G
Difficulty index	.72	.84	.85	.76	.56	.70	.70
Discrimination index	.52	.31	.27	.45	.31	.46	.51
Point biserial correlation	.53	.47	.42	.50	.26	.46	.55

Level 2, Part 1 items	A	B	C	D	E	F	G
Difficulty index	.52	.50	.51	.63	.52	.48	.63
Discrimination index	.77	.75	.80	.62	.72	.77	.54
Point biserial correlation	.58	.62	.62	.54	.60	.59	.50

Level 2, Part 2 items	A	B	C	D	E	F	G
Difficulty index	.49	.44	.50	.42	.47	.45	.59
Discrimination index	.81	.72	.72	.68	.77	.64	.71
Point biserial correlation	.61	.56	.57	.53	.61	.51	.60

Level 3, Part 1 items	A	B	C	D	E	F	G
Difficulty index	.32	.20	.37	.38	.20	.32	.35
Discrimination index	.61	.39	.70	.66	.37	.59	.69
Point biserial correlation	.52	.46	.57	.55	.46	.52	.58

Level 3, Part 2 items	A	B	C	D	E	F	G
Difficulty index	.26	.15	.21	.24	.18	.30	.30
Discrimination index	.52	.30	.41	.42	.35	.59	.54
Point biserial correlation	.51	.40	.45	.44	.42	.49	.51

Further, for the Levels Sentences the following statistics were calculated for the main sample:

Mean	22.30
Standard deviation	9.20
Kuder-Richardson 20 reliability coefficient	0.93

Diagnostic Sentences — Item Statistics

Imperatives — 1	1	2	3	4	5				
Difficulty index	.71	.62	.59	.59	.51				
Discrimination index	.48	.59	.55	.62	.71				
Point biserial correlation	.51	.49	.48	.54	.53				

Imperatives — 2	6	7	8	9	10				
Difficulty index	.63	.43	.53	.46	.44				
Discrimination index	.60	.70	.80	.72	.72				
Point biserial correlation	.54	.57	.60	.56	.58				

Questions — 1	11	12	13	14	15	16	17	18	19	20
Difficulty index	.71	.69	.65	.62	.57	.53	.41	.37	.33	.21
Discrimination index	.56	.53	.60	.59	.66	.73	.82	.70	.59	.40
Point biserial correlation	.60	.52	.59	.52	.58	.62	.65	.56	.53	.44

Questions — 2	21	22	23	24	25	26	27	28	29	30
Difficulty index	.64	.63	.48	.55	.54	.44	.34	.29	.24	.20
Discrimination index	.67	.69	.71	.70	.80	.72	.51	.52	.46	.39
Point biserial correlation	.59	.63	.54	.56	.66	.60	.42	.50	.45	.42

Negatives — 1	31	32	33	34	35	36	37	38		
Difficulty index	.67	.65	.64	.62	.59	.50	.49	.35		
Discrimination index	.65	.60	.68	.69	.70	.65	.80	.66		
Point biserial correlation	.61	.56	.64	.62	.59	.52	.61	.52		

Negatives — 2	39	40	41	42	43	44	45[1]	46		
Difficulty index	.60	.55	.63	.59	.47	.49	—	.29		
Discrimination index	.68	.71	.74	.72	.85	.79	—	.54		
Point biserial correlation	.55	.57	.66	.64	.64	.65	—	.50		

[1]No item met the statistical criteria

Phrases — 1	47	48	49	50	51	52	53			
Difficulty index	.56	.53	.50	.47	.44	.43	.40			
Discrimination index	.76	.67	.78	.63	.74	.70	.66			
Point biserial correlation	.65	.53	.61	.48	.50	.55	.53			

Phrases — 2	54	55	56	57	58	59	60			
Difficulty index	.56	.36	.17	.16	.36	.19	.38			
Discrimination index	.50	.43	.31	.32	.65	.38	.67			
Point biserial correlation	.41	.39	.42	.35	.52	.42	.56			

Clauses — 1	61	62	63	64	65	66	67	68	69	70	71
Difficulty index	.65	.50	.48	.45	.40	.40	.38	.36	.31	.32	.27
Discrimination index	.61	.77	.78	.69	.64	.58	.50	.66	.57	.49	.50
Point biserial correlation	.55	.62	.61	.56	.53	.50	.44	.54	.48	.39	.46

Clauses — 2	72	73	74	75	76	77	78	79	80	81	82
Difficulty index	.63	.44	.21	.39	.30	.38	.30	.34	.23	.27	.21
Discrimination index	.60	.73	.41	.72	.49	.67	.57	.50	.44	.46	.39
Point biserial correlation	.54	.58	.41	.55	.43	.55	.54	.47	.45	.40	.41

Field trials

Further trials were conducted with the assistance of speech therapists in the Auckland area. Two samples were used. The first consisted of 100 children drawn at random from all five-year-olds, while the second was also of 100 five-year-olds but was drawn only from children who had been referred for therapy.

Analysis of the item difficulties from these studies confirms that three distinct levels of difficulty have been obtained. This is shown graphically in Figure 1. A teacher can therefore start the administration with items from the middle difficulty level. If these are repeated correctly it is unnecessary to administer the sentences from the lower difficulty level. Since all the Level 1 sentences are of lower difficulty than those of Level 2 it can safely be assumed that the child would pass those items also. This saves considerably in administration time.

An additional outcome of the analysis was to establish that the 42 items of the Levels Sentences have a reproducibility coefficient of 0.83. This was established by Guttman Scalogram analysis. With a perfect scale one could say that if item X were repeated successfully by a child, then all the items below it would also be correctly repeated by the child. (Such a scale would have a scalability coefficient of 1.00.) The scalability of the R O L items means that very often one would be correct in predicting that a child who has demonstrated competence with grammatical structure X will also be competent with all structures which precede X on the R O L.

The trials using speech therapists as recorders are of importance in the development of the R O L. They confirm that the findings obtained under research conditions with one sample and only two recorders can be replicated with different groups of children using many different recorders under field conditions.

Fig. 1. ROL Item Difficulties from Field Trial

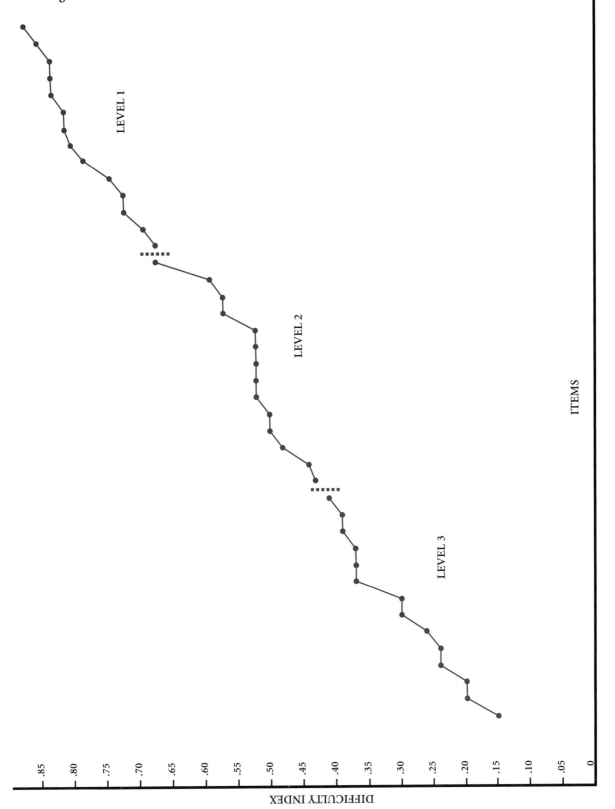

References

Bringham, T.A. and Sherman, J.A. An experimental analysis of verbal imitation in preschool children. *Journal of Applied Behaviour Analysis.* 1968, 1, 2: 151–58.

Bruner, J., Olver, Rose R. and Greenfield, Patricia M. *Studies in Cognitive Growth.* New York: Wiley, 1966.

Clay, Marie M. Sentence Repetition: Elicited Imitation of a Controlled Set of Syntactic Structures by Four Language Groups. *Monographs of the Society for Research in Child Development.* 1971, 36, 3.

Clay, M.M., Gill, M., Glynn, T., McNaughton, T. and Salmon, K. *Record of Oral Language and Biks and Gutches.* Auckland: Heinemann, 1983.

Clay, Marie M. *Biks and Gutches: Learning to Inflect English.* Auckland: Heinemann, 2007.

Dale, P.S. *Language Development: Structure and Function.* Hinsdale, Illinois: The Dryden Press, 1972.

Day, H.D. and Day, K.C. (1978). The reliability and validity of the Concepts About Print and Record of Oral Language. Resources in Education, ED179932. Arlington, Virginia: ERIC Document Reproduction Services.

Department of Education. *Language Programmes for Maori Children.* Wellington, 1972.

Edwards, R.P.A. and Gibbon, V. *Words Your Children Use.* London: Burke, 1964.

Eillebrecht, B.J. The Teaching of Language: A survey of teacher opinion. Unpublished report, 1971.

Elley, W.B. (1991). Acquiring literacy in a second language: the effects of book based programs. *Language Learning,* 41 (3): 375–411.

Fraser, C, Bellugi, U. and Brown, R.W. Control of grammar in imitation, comprehension and production. *Journal of Verbal Learning and Verbal Behaviour.* 1963, 2: 121–35.

Graham, N.C. Short-term memory and syntactic structure in educationally subnormal children. *Language and Speech.* 1968, 1: 209–19.

Harwood, F.W. Quantitive study of the speech of Australian children. *Language and Speech.* 1959, 2: 236–71.

Jordan, Christina M. and Robinson, W.P. The grammar of working and middle class children using elicited imitations. *Language and Speech.* 1972, 15, 2: 122–40.

Menyuk, Paula. *Sentences Children Use.* Cambridge, Massachusetts: MIT Press, 1969.

Osser, H., Wang, M.D. and Zaid, F. The young child's ability to imitate and comprehend speech: a comparison of two sub-cultural groups. *Child Development,* 1969, 40: 1063–75.

Pond, Sharon T. Reading Recovery and Children with Low Language Levels: An Administrative Project, Massey University, 1999.

Scott, F.S., Bowley, C.C., Brockett, C.S., Brown, J.G. and Goddard, P.R. *English Grammar: A linguistic study of its classes and structures.* Auckland: Heinemann Educational Books, 1968.

Sherman, J.A. Imitation and language development in H.W. Reese (ed.) *Advances in Child Development and Behaviour.* New York: Academic Press, 6, 1971.

Slobin, D.I. and Welsh, C.A. Elicited imitations as a research tool in developmental psycholinguistics in C.A. Ferguson and D.I. Slobin (eds) *Readings on Child Language Acquisition.* New York: Holt, Rinehart & Winston, 1973.